The Entrepreneurship Teacher Playbook:

Tested Tools for Teaching Entrepreneurship

Beau Brannan

ACKNOWLEDGMENTS

Thanks to Matt Hurdle for getting the foundation set for the class and program and also for help on the Business Problems chapter. Also deep thanks to Mike Panesis and Greg Monterrosa for being incredible supporters and encouragers of me, the program and my students.

CONTENTS

INTRODUCTION

I still remember like it was yesterday. January 4, 2006 the iconic BCS College Football National Championship at the Rose Bowl between Texas and USC. Reggie Bush, Matt Leinart, Vince Young, Pete Carroll, and Mack Brown would have been #trending but there was no iPhone, Android, Snapchat, Instagram, or Twitter in our lives. Logging onto Facebook or simply texting friends at ten cents a pop was really the only way to discuss the game in real time. In only a decade, I am now taking an Uber to watch a Rose Bowl game at a friend's house, streamed from his Apple TV, and then sending him money through Venmo for beer and DoorDash and asking "Alexa" what high school the running back attended.

When I first started teaching a class of 10th graders, one of the classes I inherited required an assignment to be turned in on a 1.44 MB floppy disk! Today, I am lucky if one or two students in a given class even knows what a floppy disk is. I know older colleagues can easily one up me with their anecdotes, but truly the technology curve has exploded in the last ten years or so. It is not a surprise that high school and college students are learning, navigating and interacting in ways radically different from students in 2006. And while this is not a new or revolutionary observation, students are rapidly adapting to technological changes while education in general is struggling to stay meaningful and relevant. Education today resembles a Blockbuster Video in a Netflix world (and even these examples will be outdated shortly). The quick fix by many educators is to teach the same old content-driven way, but with shiny new devices. I have humbly learned the Internet is always going to win the content game and as a result of this content battle, students have been losing out on developing meaningful soft skills (work ethic, communication, problem solving, grit, negotiating, time management, etc.) and left with a relatively dry, vapid imagination at graduation.

In addition to the arbitrary date of January 4th 2006, not only has technology increased and evolved rapidly, there has also been documented and substantial increases in student anxiety, depression, and suicidal tendencies. I have also seen this change myself. It seems our technology-driven and instant gratification trained culture reacts: more screen time to distract, and more convenient access to medication to numb the emotional pain. While some social scientists will declare it is still early to make a direct correlation between screens and student mental health, the duck is walking and quacking like one. I am well aware not all forms of depression and anxiety are similar and not always connected to behavior, but the increase in statistics along with the "screens" variable makes me consider how I can thoughtfully engage my students on this issue.

While briefly reflecting on the current state of technology and its impact on students, the goal of this book is not a Luddite Manifesto. I believe technology is morally neutral—it's what you do with it. A thoughtful and intentional use of technology can change lives and be a critical supplement in education and obviously in entrepreneurship. However, I am concerned about allowing technology in my life and in my student's lives without much prudence to our own peril and overall health. Human beings are not designed to be reduced to simply consuming, but are fundamentally creative, thinking, active and relational. I have discovered these can be coached and encouraged back into my student's tech-driven lives and there is a strategic opportunity to do so through the thoughtful creation of a hands-on entrepreneurship program in secondary schools.

1 THE IMPERATIVE FOR AN ENTREPRENEURSHIP CLASS

Since entrepreneurship means different things to different people, I believe an entrepreneurship program and class is not about creating a bunch of little capitalists or future shark tankers; but rather the goal is to creatively and actively engage student hearts and minds to solve real problems, to practice leadership, be bold, discover purpose and values, communicate articulately, and collaborate well with others. For many students, the current academic system rewards them for copying, mimicking and regurgitating information. Some students are also rewarded for figuring out how to game the system (arguably entrepreneurial in its own right). But it is interesting to me the Spanish word for entrepreneur is *emprendedor(a)*, someone who undertakes. This feels to me more like a proactive verb. There is meaningful and intentional action involved. It is not merely a title or something to have on a college resume or social media bio, or even something you do passively. This refreshing translation suggests the point of entrepreneurship is to courageously undertake something in order to create something new, or rethink something more intelligently.

I have several college admissions friends who find plenty of high achieving students, but lament the scarcity of students possessing resilience and substance. A great way to begin to cultivate these characteristics is by taking students seriously and giving them context-specific opportunities for leadership, courage, critical thinking and solving real problems. For me, the end goal of the entrepreneurship class is for the students to improve and develop these skills. A functioning or "successful" business at the end of the course is irrelevant and not required to receive the benefits of the class. While there is coursework to be done, the real assessments I care about are the ones which ask them the right questions, require them to critically self-evaluate and demonstrate improvement from project to project. I have already begun to see the merits of an entrepreneurship program building into students a sense of confidence, imagination, character and giving them something meaningful to work on. While I can explore these themes in a humanities class, adding entrepreneurship to the mix with some "skin in the game" and undertaking, moves the students from the ideal to the real, from being all talk, to all action. It is hard work, but it is necessary work.

2 PLAYBOOK NOTES

The ideas listed in this "playbook" are not exhaustive, nor a how-to, and not intended as lesson plans, a syllabus or curriculum. There are plenty of free entrepreneurship courses available online as well as courses on how to teach entrepreneurship from the most prestigious universities. There are many reputable "plug and play" entrepreneurship curriculums available for purchase or subscription. This playbook is simply a stream of consciousness of ideas or "plays" I have used predominantly in a secondary school setting to be considered as a supplement, or to aid in student engagement. The ideas are easily adaptable and user-friendly in both collegiate and professional settings as well as in different disciplines.

My grid for testing ideas for the class is to find something engaging, relational and context-specific. Specially, I want to create space for coaching, introduce new tools, develop skills, and ask, "would I actually enjoy or appreciate this myself?" I want to be able to take my students and their ideas seriously but more importantly build into their character and lives.

The key assumption is that the reader will be somewhat familiar with the *lean startup methodology*. There is plenty of literature and even a web search will yield a basic understanding, but Steve Blank (steveblank.com) is the best guide. Essentially, the lean method sketches out a hypothesis (idea) using a Business Model Canvas to see how a company creates value for itself and their customer. Through an iterative process and constant pivoting, the business model seeks validation by "getting out of the building" and talking to multiple customers and getting valuable feedback on a Minimum Viable Product leading to the startup proper. This researched process is much more efficient than a traditional business plan and is the context for this playbook and my journey.

There is always a weird tension of having a formal class on entrepreneurship when the entrepreneurial mindset is stereotypically anti-formal and anti-class. A student who receives an "A" in the class is not necessarily an entrepreneur. And an entrepreneur doesn't need the class to succeed. However, context is everything and I believe the discipline of entrepreneurship is not mutually exclusive with academia. In a world of backlash against overpriced college and the call to drop out and carve your own path; I have learned a well-rounded entrepreneurship course should infuse humanities so we do not detach ourselves from our own humanity in the startup process. This could very well be the last chance a student is engaged in practical moral and philosophical conversations before life hits. I always tell my students it doesn't matter if they go on to start a business or even get into the business world, but the experiences they will have in the class will make them a better person, and the skills will translate into almost anything they do. This class should be known as one which explores human potential, builds confidence, and transforms imaginations while guiding them through the lean startup/problem solving methodology. While there is always an individual dynamic, entrepreneurship is a team sport—it is meant to be played and played with others. And just as there are fundamentals and principles and rules in athletics, they do not merely exist to be studied, but are designed with action in mind. Therefore, I want to create as many opportunities to learn by doing.

In addition to all this, students appreciate an entrepreneurship class that feels "entrepreneurial" in the sense that there is not a third party "plug-n-play" curriculum leading the whole time. I get the opportunity to create and facilitate the experience, take creative risks, listen, coach and bring value to the students. My attitude and energy needs to be positive and infectious and is every bit as important as the content covered. Whether we like it or not, teaching is relational and the entrepreneurial spirit (and even the educational spirit) can be quenched in a very insincere and contrived environment.

Finally, just as a coach is not wise to force plays that do not fit the system or players, these plays are open source and very moldable to fit your context, system or student ability. Don't do something from this playbook that isn't you. There are many entrepreneurship curriculums and systems for sale out there and they all have their merits, but I believe the best experience for students is going to be one which is organic and authentic and comes from out of the instructor. This definitely means more work and preparation for the instructor, but if educators are being consistent with the realities of entrepreneurship then we should model the hard work it takes to be one. If you are creating a program from scratch in K-12, hiring the right person to lead the class is critical to its success. The teacher does not need to have business or entrepreneurial experience, but you want a nice blend of creativity and emotional intelligence in your hire. In short, whether you are an entrepreneur-in-residence or not, act like one or try to become one because teachers (no matter the subject) should be entrepreneurs in how they think about their class, the curriculum, and how they provide value to the students.

3 FIRST DAY, FIRST PLAY

The first day of class can be awkward. Some students and teachers like it, others despise it. Personally, I don't really like it because of how easy it can be cliché. Some teachers wow the students on the first day and then it all goes downhill from there. Other teachers go through the syllabus and legalese and kill the students softly. Other teachers will try and do icebreakers and do "two truths and a lie" the whole time and students are dying inside. Sometimes teachers give you their life synopsis to try and relate and/or give their credentials to justify why they have a right to teach you. I have also asked the more empathetic, 'what do you want to get out of this class?' which can be useful, but I find most students don't really know what to say the first day.

The point is, it is very difficult to pull off a great first day. A common teacher mistake is to ask general or vague questions to the class and hope students will bite a la Ben Stein in Ferris Bueller, "anyone? anyone?" An easy idea to get student opinions heard while protecting their shyness or reducing anxiety is to hand out index cards. Ask a question and then have the students anonymously write their answer down, collect, shuffle and read aloud the responses to the class. I recommend asking two questions. One being the actual question you want to ask, and then ask a goofy one or a "would you rather?" I cannot stress enough how critical humor is to a classroom environment. Students will key in very fast that the classroom is a safe space when there is healthy laughter. And laughter will be a prized asset in the entrepreneurial journey. But again, don't do something that isn't you. Students pick up on inauthenticity very quickly.

One of the first questions I like to ask is "what is the first word or image that comes to mind when you hear the word, entrepreneurship?" For the backside of the card, I might ask something like, "would you rather be the Chuck E. Cheese mascot for a day or a Chick-Fil-A mascot for the day?" Or "Who do you think is the creepiest cereal mascot and why?"

For the main question, the vast majority of answers from the students illicit things like 'money', 'freedom', 'business', 'being rich' or 'shark tank.' This is a great segue into setting up the fact entrepreneurship is actually a very difficult journey and how we tend to romanticize the success aspects. I like to use the escape scene from *The Shawshank Redemption* to illustrate the point. If you use it, know there is one use of the word, shit. The scene is Red (Morgan Freeman) narrating how Andy Dufresne (Tim Robbins) escaped Shawshank prison. The image is Andy crawling through the sewer while you hear, "Andy crawled to freedom through five hundred yards of shit smelling foulness I can't even imagine, or maybe I just don't want to..." The iconic image of Andy getting out and holding his arms up triumphantly is the connection point to the student answers. That image of the arms raised and basking in freedom is the success—it's the money and yacht and freedom and expensive homes and working for yourself. But we cannot talk about the success without tunneling through the crap. That is what entrepreneurship is—tunneling through the crap! Entrepreneurship isn't the success, it's the process, the undertaking, and you have to be okay with it. The image is powerful and is something you can draw from throughout the course when things get difficult. "Hey, remember you have to be able and willing to tunnel through the crap." I really take seriously the reality of entrepreneurship; there will be difficulties and high failure rates, and I don't want any false pretense or misleading the students about the class or entrepreneurship in general. They have to be ok with 'tunneling through the crap.' If they are not okay with that, then they should consider dropping the course.

4 "SNAKE OIL"

A fantastic warm-up game (also can be used as a first day game) and another way to build trust and a safe environment is by playing *Snake Oil*. The game is discontinued unfortunately but you can still find versions on Amazon or Ebay. If you cannot find it, you can always make your own but requires a little bit of work. Potentially fun work though! I would suggest you get a couple friends and some wine or whisky and generate as many nouns as you can on index cards. The way the game works in general is each participant is dealt five cards with one word items. For instance, milk or paste or trampoline. There is another stack of cards with a target market or customer. These cards might have teacher or astronaut or grandma. You select or draw a customer from that pile and then the players carefully select two of the five cards in their hand to create a new product for that customer. So you might group together milk and trampoline to create the "Milk-Trampoline" product for Astronauts. The players then give a quick pitch of their product/idea and how it will bring value or solve a problem for that customer. I like to ask Business Model Canvas questions such as where do I buy your product, and what is the price point? You can select the winning pitch or have the students vote. The game encourages public speaking, pitching, creativity and problem-solving. It is really fun and some students are incredibly creative with their answers. Adjust the rules if you'd like to fit your class better. Another way to do this is by having students generate random words and you write them on the board until you have about 50 words. Put the students in groups and let them pick any two words to create their product. You could assign a customer or let them identify the target market based on their words. I have also done this on a back-to-school night and the parents loved it.

5 CHARACTER AND INTEGRITY

I personally feel a sense of obligation to begin each class with a very short thought or quote or reflection on character since I believe the true measuring stick for me as a teacher is how many lives I can positively invest into. This can feel forced and out of place if not setup properly. The setup I share with students is how easily a lifetime of success can be ripped and rendered meaningless by one lapse in judgment. It doesn't take too much looking around to find anecdotes both past and in recent news to support this. As students build into their business or bottom-line, they cannot neglect investing into their character. I personally believe there is an eternal quality to it, but that is my opinion. On a smaller scale, I want to instill in the students a sense of 'corporate social responsibility' and integrity into all their decisions. There is no doubt a cost of compliance, but more times than not it actually ends up being a huge benefit and gain in the long run and it is the right thing to do. I have failed if a student became a billionaire at the expense of exploiting people in a third world country, or by dehumanizing their employees. While these issues get discussed later as they consider their startup's missions and values, having wisdom in the bank so to speak only enhances the conversation later.

This character segment does not need to be preachy or long at all, but it is always one of the first things I do when starting class. I have been known to simply put up a Proverb from the Bible or a quote on a slide and read it aloud (unpack it if necessary), give a few seconds of silence to let it sink in and then I move on. I then give them the full list of Proverbs or quotes at the end of the course to have. Surprisingly, many students are grateful to have it and sometimes ask for another copy.

The other option (which can be done as a Twitter poll question or through anonymous notecards again) is by asking Scruples. Scruples are ethical dilemma questions and can easily be tailored to your class and can be both fun, enlightening, and also depressing. It is published as a board game and so feel free to peruse Amazon or eBay for a set. You may have to pick through the cards for more business related questions. If you do not feel comfortable facilitating a character portion of the class, then simply asking the students to write down 2-3 things they are grateful for to begin class or have them write in their *Five Minute Journal* (available on Amazon, or make your own) can also yield positive changes in their hearts and mindset.

If you have the ability and time and confidence to incorporate a more intentional humanities approach in your class (see Humanities Approach for ideas), it will not be a waste.

6 EGG DROP AND AGILE SPRINT

There are several fun icebreaker and team building type games and simulations available out there and can easily be found by doing a web search. A common and popular one is the "marshmallow tower". In 18 minutes, teams compete to build the tallest free-standing structure using only: 20 sticks of spaghetti, 3 feet of tape of tape, 3 feet of string, and a marshmallow (medium to big). The marshmallow must be on the very top, everything else is fair game. The debriefing after they build their towers is where the real learning begins. You can ask students about their initial thought process, assumptions they made, and how everyone felt (were they heard, or ignored, or did they even participate, and why/why not), and finally how they would go about it differently if they attempted it again. It is definitely a fun activity. I like to play the "diamond music" song, Palladio by Karl Jenkins which is about 3:45 followed up by Ravel's Bolero. Together it is a little bit longer than 18 minutes but the music creates a sense of urgency as it repeats and gets louder until it crescendos. I get a kick when students ask about Bolero, "what is the deal with this song?" or "what are you doing to us?"

However, one project I have found to be very effective and addresses several concepts is the egg drop. But this is not your old science class egg drop. The goal is through an agile design sprint method, build an egg drop protecting apparatus where eggs may be dropped from a second or third floor without breakage using limited materials and a set budget. I do not let the students pick their own team because it is early in the class and I want them to get comfortable with being uncomfortable. An easy way is to use a randomizer online (random.org/lists), but I am too lazy to input names so I like to scatter a bunch of old baseball cards on the floor and have them pick one. Teams will be grouped either by the team name (Tigers, Reds, Expos, etc.) or you can match by card design (89 Topps) or some other variation. Old baseball cards are cheap to get on eBay or at a garage sale if you don't have them laying around. But you can use anything (Playing Cards, Garbage Pail Kids, Pokémon, candy, or create your own).

Once in teams they are given a limited amount of materials to choose from and a budget. I am the market so they may only buy from me. I use Word and grab a purchase order template and customize it. I require the teams to fill one out every time they make a purchase from me. They could buy several items at once, but if they came to me two minutes later asking for one more order of tape, I make them fill out another form. The groans are music to my ears. I am not a masochist, but the world runs on paper trails and I also want them to be more thoughtful about planning for their needs. In the real world, materials aren't always available on the spot.

I also strongly encourage the students to seek prototype validation and data. In other words, I stress they need to do multiple tests and this is all part of their budgeting. The only drop that counts is the official live drop when they pitch in front of me. (See the Appendix for the Egg-Drop Handout)

If you have more time, incorporating *Sprint: How to Solve Big Problems and Test New Ideas in Just Five Days* (gv.com/sprint/) will be helpful. Teaching the agile design sprint early is really critical for subsequent projects and also from a practical perspective since the discipline of agile project management is considered a best practice in many business settings. I usually do not have the time to unpack the *Sprint* book and so instead of note-taking or extensive lectures, I teach this method through the egg-drop by resetting each step each day of the sprint. There is definitely flexibility in the sprint steps and you can combine a couple steps in one 'day' or class, but this is a basic sketch of my edited process and also gives a basic introductory understanding and benefit of this lean startup tool.

The first step is identifying the problem. In most cases I have already done so, but I still have them verbalize and articulate it. I stress the need for a contraption which will allow someone to drop eggs safely from the second or third story. I am clear to them that I am the investor so they need to show me some upside or scalability in their product beyond a one-off. They are tempted to have a very low price point to compete against other groups and I do not question their decision until the debrief, unless they ask me directly.

The second step is to simply ideate. Write a list of all the different ways to build an egg-drop. They are not allowed to self-edit or edit others. In other words, many times we have a default to quickly say, 'oh that won't work...nevermind' I encourage them on this day of the sprint, it does not matter. If it involves a time machine, a garden gnome, or a cat then it is still fair game. The ideation process is also helpful because I think it is human nature to jump right into things and there are of course situations where immediate action is called for, but when investing time and money into a project it is wise and efficient to have explored all options and develop a game plan. I encourage students that oftentimes it is the odd ideas that are often much closer to a viable product than you think.

The third step or third day is to decide/vote on a design and sketch out their user story. I hand out 3 different types of stickers and require *every* student to vote on their list of ideas. The red sticker stands for "no way." The yellow sticker stands for "it has merit, but not quite the best" and the green sticker is "this is the one." I always check in with the groups before they start sketching the blueprint. I want to push back on the students who say, "whatever" or, "it's fine" on a design as they try to come to group consensus. Since it is early in the course, some students haven't found their voice yet and I want them to be able to communicate why they have their viewpoint. Surprisingly, there are occasional "12 Angry Men" moments and the group flips their design idea because a student finally felt empowered to share their reasoning. Once there is genuine consensus, they need to sketch out each step of the building process. At first, students don't appreciate this step, but I tell them they all have a different mental model currently. This step is critical because one student might be thinking of using two pieces of string and another envisions four. Sketching out the steps prevents this disconnect and helps them properly budget. I encourage them to think of it as a roadmap or recipe on how to build the contraption exactly and precisely.

Step 4 or day 4 is prototyping and testing. This is where they finally build and test their product. It is up to you if you want them to have a minimum amount of drops. Sometimes it can be a useful teaching tool to wait until the debrief to ask why they felt only doing one or two drops was enough to validate their product.

Finally Step 5 is the live drop and pitch. Students pitch to me their company name, the name of the product, all the features and benefits of their egg drop apparatus, cost and price point. They can live-drop as they pitch or after their pitch. I then usually ask questions about their product (which is fun to see which students step up in defending their product). Some aspects students neglect to think about are: their labor costs, the ability to drop more than one egg, and the removal of the egg being simple (some student projects take like two minutes to unravel).

Again, the debrief is where the real learning starts to happen as they make connections. They always want to know who had the best egg drop product and of course they should be acknowledged, but there could also be a group that you, the investor, is most interested in. In other words, as you debrief and ask the group questions about their process and why they did what they did, you can begin to affirm their collaboration and even if they didn't have the 'winning egg drop' you could award them the contract based on their thought process and teamwork. After all, many VC's are more interested in investing in the person or team than the actual idea itself.

Finally, if the Sprint method is not something you want to explore, doing the egg drop by going through the steps of the Business Model Canvas is a fantastic way to teach the framework though a practical project.

7 CLASS TEXTS

Depending on your class layout there are several entrepreneurship books worth using as a text. Here is a short-list of recommendations for texts or supplemental reading:

The Four Steps to the Epiphany, Steve Blank
E-Myth Revisited, Michael Gerber
Business Model Generation: A Handbook for Visionaries, Game Changers, and Challengers, Alexander Osterwalder
The Entrepreneur Rollercoaster, Darren Hardy
The Lean Startup, Eric Reis
Zero to One, Peter Thiel
Start Something that Matters, Blake Mcycoskie
Let My People Go Surfing, Yvon Chouinard

Personally, I use *Setting the Table* by Danny Meyer in the first part of the course. I use it because it serves as an incredible connecting point for the students since restaurants and restaurant experiences are not lost on them. Meyer weaves personal stories, anecdotes, lessons learned with sound business advice. Most importantly is his emphasis on hospitality in business and believe it or not, this is actually a novel concept for many younger students. It helps them to think about their customer more thoughtfully and builds a solid foundation for lean startup customer validation. I typically have the students read one chapter at a time and email me one salient point which made them think, something they would like to implement now, or in their future business and why. This also reduces the workload and stress for them. I like to create a separate Gmail account and request the reading be sent there. The organizational options in Gmail are perfect and you don't have to worry about separating out your Olive Garden spam with student responses.

In class we do a quick overview of the chapter once a week and I like to curate some of the best responses from students to read in class. This is easy to do when you request a short response from them. You can share their responses either anonymously or publicly. In general, having the answers in advance allows an opportunity for engagement, especially with more quiet students. In other words, you can say "Tara, I really liked your comment on the employee stakeholder having more value than an investor stakeholder; could you maybe talk a little more about why you felt that was important?" This can engage a student who normally wouldn't raise their hand or speak their mind. Since you have already validated their voice it shouldn't be too hard for them to annotate their idea further.

In the second part of the course, I use *Disciplined Entrepreneurship* by Bill Aulet. This is the de facto text for me and can be as rigorous or as simplified as you need. I use this in conjunction with the student start-up project so they have another 'mentor' in the process. (See the Student Startup for its full implementation). A practical organizer of the book is available at detoolbox.com or you can spring for the accompanying workbook (*Disciplined Entrepreneurship Workbook*, Bill Aulet). I will have students not only read and discuss the text in class, but also complete the steps on the website as a way to make sure they didn't miss anything in the book.

8 CLASS FORMATIONS

Something doesn't feel right when you start class by just letting them 'get to work.' I have also learned project focus does not last a full class session. I will therefore 'prime the pump' and front-load the class. I will do this each day but usually with a different focus or topic. I start by sharing what we are doing that day and then begin with the character Proverb or quote and then depending on the day, I will move onto one or a combination of the following topics:

"Goats"

Goats (greatest of all time) is where I will read aloud a carefully selected interview of a successful entrepreneur to the class (5-8 minutes). I require them to simply find one idea which grabs them and write it down. They are allowed to write more, but I require at least one. I also use this "find one thing" method because many times students get overloaded with information or tend evaluate and judge talks and lectures as a whole. I share with them if you can go to a conference or a speech or anything and come away with one idea, it's been worth your time. This mindset also starts to move us away from our tendency to being critical to a posture of gratitude (much easier when we are actively looking for something positive). I also make it mandatory that they physically write it down. The research points to using a different part of the brain when we write, and that part of the brain wants to do a better job remembering the point. Some students insist on their laptop, but I hold my ground and I tell them they can type it in afterwards. I have them write their point(s) down on yellow legal pad paper or equivalent in order to make it have a significance. They seem to get into a certain mode when the yellow paper is out and they have pen in hand. Afterwards, I ask the students to volunteer which concept stuck out to them the most. This is one of those few times where I can ask a general question ("so what concept stuck out the most?") and I always get participation even though they don't get points for it. The source material I draw from mostly is *Tools of Titans* by Tim Ferriss. I curate about 25 of my favorite sections and read those interviews. At the end of each semester I have the students pick the idea that was most poignant, or one that they have started to implement or would like to implement. I call on each student and have them share. I end up learning a lot about my students and what is important to them or what they feel is lacking in their lives. Students regularly cite this exercise as one of their favorites in the class. The key is to keep encouraging them that the concepts or advice they resonate with are great, but they have to be able to put it into practice otherwise they just have a nice yellow paper with words on it. If you have the ability to coach them further, go for it.

Class Readings

One day out of the week is where we discuss the assigned reading. (see Class Texts)

Personal Finance

This can be one of the more scary things to teach, especially if you yourself are not too well-versed in personal finance. It is totally ok! You are not investing their money nor are you claiming to be a CFP. I stress that I am only giving them a 30,000 foot view and I encourage them to talk to their parents (or if it is an adult group, encourage an advisor) if they want to investigate further. If you wonder what place this has in an entrepreneurship class, I believe if they cannot be good stewards of their own finances then what makes us think they will be good stewards of corporate or startup finances? Even if someone plans to outsource accounting, you still need to know what to look for. This time always proves to be fruitful as I usually get a handful of students who 'come alive' when we talk about this content. The main point and objective if nothing else is that they start the discipline of saving TODAY versus a habit of spending. I also find this habit spills into other parts of their lives as they begin to think twice about the things they consume. Don't be afraid if they ask a question and you don't know the answer. I tell them, "I don't know, let me write it down and I will get back to you." And then I find out and get back to them. This does not diminish my expertise or authority in any way, it only increases respect, plus I end up learning a lot. I recommend *The Only Investment Guide You'll Ever Need*, Andrew Tobias or *Millionaire Teacher: The Nine Rules of Wealth You Should Have Learned in School*, Andrew Hallam if you want to brush up or use as a supplement.

Here are some of the modules (roughly 10-15 minutes each) and the general talking points I use:

1. Compound Interest, Banks: Savings and Checking Accounts

Here is a great question to start with: "would you rather get 3 million dollars cash right now or a penny that doubles for 31 days?" Usually, students are astute to know there is probably a catch so they choose the penny option but don't know why.

Here is the math and the chart I put up:

Day 1: $.01
Day 2: $.02
Day 3: $.04
Day 4: $.08
Day 5: $.16
Day 6: $.32
Day 7: $.64
Day 8: $1.28
Day 9: $2.56
Day 10: $5.12
Day 11: $10.24
Day 12: $20.48
Day 13: $40.96
Day 14: $81.92
Day 15: $163.84
Day 16: $327.68

Day 17: $655.36
Day 18: $1,310.72
Day 19: $2,621.44
Day 20: $5,242.88
Day 21: $10,485.76
Day 22: $20,971.52
Day 23: $41,943.04
Day 24: $83,886.08
Day 25: $167,772.16
Day 26: $335,544.32
Day 27: $671,088.64
Day 28: $1,342,177.28
Day 29: $2,684,354.56
Day 30: $5,368,709.12
Day 31: $10,737418.24

The main point is the "miracle" of compound interest and how critical it is to start today. The 3 Million cash is absolutely the move until Day 30! If students wait until they get a "real job" or out of college to start saving they actually miss out on a lot even though they are still young. Yes, I do tell them that this return is not a realistic return and an 8-10% return is more what to expect over the long haul. It is also up to you if you want to also explain the Rule of 72. I also give them a perspective on how expensive things like a daily Starbucks latte are annually and how "a penny saved is a penny earned."

It can be hard to start the discipline of saving if you don't have a place to put the money. Sure, your mattress could work but you might as well get some interest out of it. Besides, if you aren't disciplined knowing there is money in your mattress means you have really easy access to your cash. I also go over the difference between a checking account and a savings account and stress that when you give money to the bank, it is not tucked away in a vault waiting for you. They take your money and loan it out to others to make money on your money. They will graciously give you less than 1% annual interest for the honor. Finally, because there are plenty of memes about how students learn the quadratic equation but cannot write a check, I create fake checks and have them properly fill it out. Now they know.

2. Consumer Debt

The credit card talk. I explain what credit cards are, how expensive the money you are borrowing is and how long it takes you to pay off if you just pay the minimum amount (there are several online calculators to demonstrate this). If they are in high school, I will tell them about how they will start to be bombarded with credit card offers either on their college campus or their favorite store in exchange for a free gift or 15% off their purchase and to be very cautious of these offers. I also explain merchant service fees also known as the amount charged to actually run or swipe the card. Not all cards are created equal and a credit card number swiped costs different than a card typed in manually as does a credit card tied to your checking account compared to a premium rewards card. These costs are usually a forgotten aspect in business financial models and students wonder why they only received $97 for something they sold for $100. I briefly explain the other side where having a credit card can help build credit for making bigger purchases (like cars and homes) down the road.

3. Taxes

I usually grab an old pay stub and black out my name and employer and say here is an example I found. I then walk through all the different taxes and what they mean and about the rough percentage that gets taken out of a paycheck. I have them fill out a W-4 for fun and I briefly explain exemptions as well as what a W-2 and a 1099 is, and to be aware they have to be more proactive about taxes with a 1099. I teach the students to be aware of the type of employee they are and to always remember if your first job is offering $15/hour, you are not really getting $15 an hour so don't spend it in advance.

4. Stocks

If a company wants to raise some money they have several options. One of them is to offer equity to the public. A company will offer a set amount of shares initially to raise the capital they need. This is called the Initial Public Offering. The company gets their money, and any trading afterwards is what other people are willing to pay for those shares or partial ownership of that company. The stock value therefore is essentially what people think it is worth to own a share in that company. It fluctuates based on the news and financial reports. I quickly demonstrate how to read a stock table, define some basic terms like penny stocks and day trading. Depending on how much time you have, you can always incorporate a stock market game, but I tend to encourage students to get started on their own with real money.

5. Index, Mutual Funds and ETF's

Essentially this is an investment in a group or collection of stocks with the intent of diversifying and spreading out risk; or if you cannot afford one share of Google, you can still invest in Google by getting into a mutual fund which gives you exposure (although fractionally). I introduce them to Morningstar (morningstar.com) explain NAV (net asset value) as well as some other labels with a focus on fees. Fees will eat away at potential growth and hinder the compounding effect.

6. Option Contracts: going long and selling short

This one is a little more advanced so don't bother with it if you don't understand it. The basic overview is that investors can 'bet' that a stock will go up in the future or will go down in the future. There has to be someone on the other side so it becomes a zero-sum game: one winner and one loser. If you think a stock is going up, you buy a contract for a fee (non-refundable) to say you will buy 100 shares at $100 this March 15th. This means that on March 15th if the stock goes up (like you knew it would) to $200, you have the option (but not obligation) to buy those 100 shares for $100. So you get $20,000 of stock for the price of $10,000 minus whatever you paid for the contract. To make things even more interesting, you can sell that contract to someone else before the date. Conversely, if you think a stock is going down, you can essentially borrow 100 shares at $100 each and by the March 15th date get rid of the overpriced shares and return the 100 shares back to the owner. In this case the shares are now worth $50. You borrowed $10,000 worth of shares and returned them at $5,000. The contract was about the shares not their value, so you are plus $5,000 (minus contract fees).

7. 401K/Retirement

Retirement seems like science fiction for young students, but I like to walk back the compound interest discussion and stress that while they are worried about passing Spanish class today, the day will come very fast where they are given an open enrollment seminar from HR to sign up for dismemberment insurance and their 401k. When you are young and maybe even in a lot of college debt there is a temptation to take home all of your paycheck. I tell them whatever they do to make sure they participate in their company 401k (or 403b), especially if they match. Do what is necessary to meet what they match. Finally, make sure you get a second opinion on investment options for your 401k before the broker of record pushes you into a high fee target date fund or equivalent.

8. Insurance (P&C/Financial)

I give a quick overview of how insurance works. I talk briefly about car insurance and home insurance. I then discuss life insurance (term and whole) and follow up with how Indexed Universal Life policies (and its cousin the Variable) work (combination insurance and investment into an index fund) and what to be mindful of when approached with these products (hint: fee heavy!). I then explain annuities (give the insurance company a lump sum of money and they will guarantee a percentage back to you annually) and the pros and cons of having them later in life.

9. Bonds, CD's

I refer to these as "unsexy securities" because their yields are not always exciting like stocks can be. I go over Treasuries, government/municipal and corporate bonds. I discuss how bonds are inextricably tied to interest rates and what to be aware of if you get a bond, especially if you plan to sell it prior to its maturity date. I quickly explain Certificate of Deposits where if you are perhaps not too disciplined or tempted to take money out of your savings account, you can lock it away so to speak for a little bit more interest than a savings account.

If time, I bring outside speakers for cryptocurrency, how to buy a car, and how a mortgage works.

Q&A

This is absolutely worth the time invested and is a student favorite. Once a week or so depending on course length *each* student gets a chance to be 'interviewed.' I call it Q&A because the term interview can feel overwhelming for some. I do this because I believe everybody is interesting and way too many times we never get a chance to really get to know a fellow student or colleague in our flood of to-do lists. Or we are simply content to label them in a one dimensional way. I have the students sit up front in a comfortable chair and I begin with a *hyperthetical.* Chuck Klostermann wrote some brilliant questions which are much more thought-provoking than your traditional small talk. They are extreme hypothetical questions, hence *hypertheticals.* You can purchase a set of cards on Amazon, possibly at a local bookseller or find some questions online. Make sure you read through the questions before you use them. You may need to update examples (there are some slightly outdated pop-culture references) or catch the few cards which are a little invasive and inappropriate. Most of them are just fine as written. I also like to open up the question to the other students in the class which changes the vibe to more of a cocktail party. Once that question is exhausted, I then have a quick segment called Acceptable in the 80's. This is an 80's pop culture question (you could use whatever works for you). Since I have students born after 2000 now, there is really no reason for them to know anything about 80's pop culture and so it becomes a random guess. It's fun to see the students get into it and explain the rationale for their guess. The effort you put into this is up to you. I always find a clip on YouTube to play first before I ask the question so they can enjoy the context, the hair, the synth, or whatever.

For instance, I did one on Magnum P.I. I showed the intro to the show and asked a multiple choice question about the TV show. One student came to me a week later and said, "I told my dad about the Acceptable in the 80's question about Magnum P.I. and then he told me to wait...he went into the garage and pulled out a bunch of tapes and a tape player. I didn't even know we had one. He made me watch like 5 episodes of Magnum PI with him." I was dying. Solid father-daughter bonding right there.

Finally, we end with rapid-fire questions where I ask about 10 questions and they are encouraged to answer as quickly as possible. The attitude should be hospitable as they are giving answers and testing their vulnerability in some cases. Again, I draw heavily from Tim Ferriss' questions. Feel free to add, subtract, modify your own. Here are the questions I have liked to use:

1. When you think of the word successful, who is the first person that comes to mind and why?
2. What is the thing or experience you recommend to people the most?
3. What is something you believe that other people think is insane?
4. What is your favorite documentary?
5. What purchase of $100 or less has positively impacted your life?
6. What topic would you speak about if you were asked to give a TED talk?
7. Do you have a quote you live life by or think of often?
8. What is worst advice you hear being given to you or your friends?
9. Is there anything really weird that happens to you on a regular basis?
10. If you could ask us anything or leave us with any parting thought or question, what would it be?

I have even had guests or former students drop by and the students will say, "ask them the questions!" I also will put myself in the chair at the end of the course, which they appreciate as well.

Market Watch

If you like to follow the news then you can parlay that into a quick Market Watch discussion. I typically choose things which are interesting and relevant to the students. I will be more likely to talk about Snapchat's notable news and decisions as opposed to Johnson & Johnson news. This is not because one is more important than the other, but if you want to involve more students, it is much easier when it is a topic they care or know about. You can also do a quick poll question (use ProProfs or polleverywhere.com on their thoughts). When Toy R Us announced bankruptcy, I asked the students if they thought "Toys" would reinvent themselves, or if brick and mortar toy stores have no place in today's economy. I do not always use this but it is a nice "play" to run and it gives you a chance to see who are the economists and investors in the room. If you have the ability, *The Wall Street Journal* offers incredible educator discounts and I incorporate WSJ quite often.

After any one of these fast moving opening segments, I will move into a quick Daily Stand-Up, if possible.

9 DAILY HUDDLE (STAND-UP)

The daily stand-up is a best practice in an agile environment. It is meant to be quick and efficient. I require every student to stand up and remain standing (some students will like to sit down after their turn, but it is important to emphasize listening to each other). The questions are simple:

- What did you work on yesterday (or last class)
- What are you working on today?
- Finally, anything standing in your way of accomplishing the project sprint?

I will usually leave the third one optional for time reasons, but this can be a very productive question if you have the time. The trick here is to move fast, but also make sure the students are very specific with their goals and timeframe. It is typical for a student to say, "Oh, I am going to work on the deck today" or "I am going to create some new designs" or "I am going to interview some people." Ask them specifically what part of the deck, or exactly how many designs they will complete by the end of the day, or how many interviews, etc. I always repeat (to the point of annoyance) *if you do not set a specific goal with a specific deadline you will not do it.* Period. This exercise and the teacher's willingness to fight through their vague generalities requiring specifics and deadlines will improve their ability to communicate, in addition to the practical nature of learning how to actually follow through. This is also another form of group accountability as students are verbalizing their tasks and can be 'called out' politely by their peers if they are getting distracted. I will not always use this every single day, but I will at the beginning of a project or when I sense some project fatigue.

10 THE BLE

After the dust has settled with a new class and we have done the egg drop, I introduce a new project and I introduce the BLE or Business License Exam. This is a test I created which requires a passing score of at least 80%. Since some students will likely become licensed professionals, this will be their first taste into the world of licensed exams. Students are not allowed to sell in their next project until they pass this exam. The terms are all entrepreneurial or business terms the students should know and be conversant with. The terms change and evolve all the time but I typically I will give a list of 100 terms they need to know (to see one of the versions see the Appendix: BLE). However, I do not offer them a source to find the definitions, nor do I give them lectures on the terms. They have to figure it out and find a way. It is "tunneling through the crap." Perseverance is one of the many unspoken soft skills they get a chance to test or develop. Many students will flock to Quizlet, but the nature of the questions are not straight memorization but more application.

Here is a sample question:

The North American Widget Company in their third quarter report told investors that they are "in the black." This means:

A.   they are running a deficit
B.   they are in danger of bankruptcy
C.   they are profitable
D.   their gross income is positive

The answer is C. As you can see the answers are all reasonable especially if you don't know the term. But this also tests their knowledge of gross vs net as well as "in the black."

I use ProProfs (proprofs.com) to set up the online test. The questions and answers may be set to be jumbled and random. I have created a bank of questions from the 100 terms but they are only asked 50, so no two tests are exactly the same and it reduces the chance of 'gaming the test' and memorizing answers as opposed to actually knowing it. I also do not show the correct answer. This drives the students crazy but you will be surprised how effective it is in their mastery. I require them to take the test on their device or laptop in class. Of course if this is a technological roadblock or proctoring nightmare, you can also create a hardcopy test. I would then recommend you use ZipGrade (an app-driven scantron zipgrade.com) to make life easier on you.

I always suggest the best way for them to study is to talk to a parent or friend currently in business and talk through the terms. It is a difficult test. The average student takes 4-5 attempts to pass and roughly 35-40 minutes for their first attempts, and then gets down to about 15 minutes on their final run. The crux again is that they are not allowed to start their business (specifically selling) until everyone in their group has passed. Many students begin to learn new things about themselves and other people. When we debrief later there is this huge epiphany that the only thing that stood in their way to start the business was this test. Sometimes in life there is one thing we need to do in order to move forward and we keep putting it off. Why? The lessons behind the mastery and formal assessment of the material is discovering their resourcefulness in finding answers, their goal-setting, time management, and resilience if they fail one or multiple times. You learn a lot about the students who miss the cut-off by one question two or three times in a row and keep their resolve. The frustration teaches a fantastic lesson, especially for students not accustomed to failure. Some students will approach me and seek to understand a concept and I never turn them away. I only equivocate if they ask me for the correct answer straight up.

Finally, I like to create a little certificate with their name on it when they pass. Again, Word has templates ready to go. It seems like a small gesture, but you will be surprised how triumphant it feels and appreciative they are when they earn it. It is like a trophy. To keep these concepts fresh, I like to also create trivia games based on the concepts with quizizz.com and occasionally have a quiz competition.

11 THE $20 PROJECT

This project is very worthwhile and fun (see Appendix: $20 Project), but can be difficult to pull off because we are dealing with real money and more money means more bureaucratic problems. The goal is to put students into teams again, but give them $20 and tell them to start a mini-business...go! You could choose $10 or $5 (the amount is not that important) because they are trying to start a business with limited funding. Or, you could give each team a random item and encourage them to play a game of "bigger and better." If you haven't played before, it is simply a trading game. Students are given an item, commissioned to go to strangers/neighbors and ask if they can trade their item for something bigger and better than what they have. This can create all sorts of fun lessons about cold calling, communication, hearing "no", teamwork, but also negotiation. Let's say they start with a coffee mug and end up with a nice golf club driver. They can try and sell that club and use the money for their startup capital.

For simplicity, I usually offer the money as a 0% interest loan. It must be repaid. I also will not allow them to put in their own money or ask other people for money. The only other money they can use in their business is reinvesting their profits. It is up to the teacher's discretion to allow assets such as an already owned piece of equipment. I usually go on a case by case basis.

I purposely stay out of this project in terms of managing and it is probably one of the hardest things to do. I want them to do all the figuring out and own their decisions and learn from those decisions. I want them to metaphorically skin their knee and bloody their nose. There are many times I want to step in and save them, but I hang back for their benefit. I have seen groups walk into a failure because they didn't account for something simple like sales tax, and I kept my mouth shut. I don't refuse to answer questions or give advice if they ask, but I will not volunteer anything.

The only things I require are a set of bylaws up front (see Appendix: Bylaws), a business model canvas, all of their documentation (receipts, income, etc.), and an in-class pitch presentation before they start selling and at the end. Some ways to frame this with school administration or with schools with "no student businesses allowed" is that this an educational experience, short-term (about a month), regulated in the sense that the instructor knows what the students are selling and when, and the last concern is always what will happen with the profits. Typically, the students agree on a charitable cause. Therefore this takes on more of a fundraiser vibe but with all the requirements and experience of running a small business. One year, our students donated their profits to a fellow teacher battling cancer. The decision was completely their own and it was beautiful.

One of the teachable moments that emerges when the project is over is their lack of bookkeeping. This opens up an opportunity to share some tools and resources and best practices for keeping track of expenses and bookkeeping. I find this to be way more effective and connects better than doing a standalone and disconnected lecture prior to the project.

12 RETROSPECTIVE

The retrospective is another agile best practice tool to use at the end of a project or iteration. I use ProProfs (proprofs.com) for this activity to create a quick survey. Having the student responses in advance allows you the chance to craft better questions for them in class in order to reflect further or clarify their responses. In general the questions I ask are simple:

- What went well (as a group and personally)?
- What didn't go well (as a group and personally)?
- What lessons did you learn about yourself and from your project?

If this is an on-going project with benchmarks then you can add a question about roadblocks. You could therefore reframe the question and ask "what didn't go well and/or what roadblocks did you encounter during the project?"

I will print out or have the responses handy and begin to follow-up with every student. I will ask them to either elaborate on their responses or ask some variation on the following:

- If you were CEO, what would you do differently?

- Specifically, what will you do differently in the next project?
- What was different from your participation in the first project compared to the second project?
- What exactly was your role?
- Do you feel the workload was fairly distributed?

As you most likely will encounter, the two biggest problems students cite are lack of communication and time management. Be willing to press in and ask further, "so how could you have improved the communication?" Or "Why was the time management not effective? How could you have improved it?" "How will you change this for the next project?"

The retrospective is critical because typically the reasons for failure or ineffectiveness is usually not just one cause. Our minds want to simplify it to one reason but there are actually several. The "retro" allows for students to see the complex nature of a startup, the value of reflection, measuring growth, the perspective of others on their team, and more importantly resilience. I encourage them to not make the same mistakes or flaws in the next iteration or project and give them permission to create new mistakes.

13 REJECTION THERAPY

Outside of team projects, rejection therapy is a fun assignment and the students always enjoy it. The idea is derived from Jia Jiang and others but I will use Jia's experience to set it up (rejectiontherapy.com/100-days-of-rejection-therapy/).

I show the class Jia Jiang's video where he decides to go to Krispy Kreme to ask for donuts made in the shape of the Olympic rings. After the video, I tell the class they get a chance to do something similar. The objective is to come up with an opportunity to engage a stranger and ask a request that you are pretty sure you will receive a "no" answer. The idea behind the assignment is that by going in expecting a "no" and taking the risk anyways will foster a tolerance and hopefully an inoculation for rejection and increase their boldness. Students have said they feel more emboldened and confident as a result of the exercise. I ask the students to film it discreetly so we can all watch it together in class (which is another form of rejection therapy). The most interesting aspect are the times when students actually hear a "yes" answer. I had one student go to Taco Bell to order a Baja Blast "slushie." He then asked the employee if he could go behind the counter and fill it up himself. The employee looked around and then waved him over. The student slid over the counter and filled up his cup and quickly slid back over the counter to pay. Absolutely hysterical. Many times they are not prepared for the yes answer which raises another discussion about how to be prepared for success.

Exercise caution as some students may want to push the legal boundaries, so go ahead and establish upfront that doing things like: robbing a bank or trying to buy alcohol as a minor are not permitted—both for class and in life. The other thing to be mindful of are filming rules. Encourage students to talk to the people involved afterwards to seek their permission. It won't be posted publicly, it is purely for class.

One last piece of advice: many students will just try and go to McDonalds and ask for something for free like an ice cream cone (assuming the machine isn't broken) so try and encourage something a little more innovative or creative beyond asking for freebies.

14 CONTINUING EDUCATION

"Number one failure of CEO's? They don't read enough!" - Tom Peters

There is a glut of content, books, articles, podcasts, documentaries and TV shows for insight and inspiration about the entrepreneurial journey. While an instructor always has their items to recommend, I believe the students should have a choice too. In my years teaching, assigned reading is always an uphill drive in the snow. But when a student has say, the uphill is still uphill, but at least you have snow chains. I like to assign anywhere from 3-5 of these "Continuing Education" assignments or CE's. It is very simple, I ask them to locate an article or listen to a podcast or even watch an episode of Shark Tank of their choice and submit about a 250-word response on what the content was about and then discuss the biggest takeaway for them personally and why and how they will apply it. This can also be a great way to discover new content for the instructor which could eventually turn into required reading, but you can also read between the lines sometimes and discover what the student is interested in, especially when they are unsure. It also is intended to instill the importance of reading.

Another possible angle is to require they post on their own blog or some other form of social media to get used to putting themselves and their ideas out there. I do not do this because I have learned less is more and asking them to do this is not productive, but if this fits your strengths—especially if you are very seasoned with social media and blogging, then it might be a great assignment and coaching opportunity.

15 ELEVATOR "PITCH" MUSIC

Music in the classroom is underrated. I typically use music when students enter the room and during dedicated project times. The key is to find music which is not too loud or grating. I have found music relatively unknown and unfamiliar works best. You can also try and give up the "aux" to students if you want to try it. It is a bigger deal to them than you think, but make sure your rules are clear. You can also create a shareable playlist on Spotify where students can add songs to the playlist. I am probably fooling myself but so far I have not had complaints when I have the "aux." My go-to playlists on Spotify are: the Danger Mouse Jukebox (updated regularly), Adult Swim Bumps, and ISO50.

Another fun idea I have implemented and the students really enjoy is the use of a walk-up song. If this concept is foreign to you, the walk up song is the song of choice (usually in baseball, but also in boxing or wrestling) where a player will have their 'pump up song' played as they walk up to bat or into the ring. You could use this when it is their turn for Q&A or any other moment you see fit. It takes a little bit of effort to set up, but the students can't stop talking about it. The way it works is you ask them to submit their personal walk up (or pump up) song. There are different ways to organize this, but the easiest on you is to have the students pre-cut their 30 second song clip and send it to you. You can rename the file to their name for easy use. Expect tech issues on their end, but it's worth it and for many students it is their first experience editing and will give them some technical confidence moving forward.

16 LEGOS AND EVERYTHING IS AWESOME

Legos are an incredible way to get students engaged and involved. I have watched students completely forget about their phones as they dive into the Legos to build. High school, college and adult students all benefit from the kinesthetic learning. The task I like to assign is for them to construct a model of their idea, product, or service and explain a user story with it. To start, have the students build something simple like a cat or a duck. Give them a few minutes to build and then have them show their model and pitch/share/explain how they have a cat, etc. Many students will keep it simple: "this is the head, this is the tail." I encourage them to be descriptive and draw the audience into the model by storytelling and giving details, names, colors and context.

After the simple build, I will have them create a model of a typical day at school. Again, this is an opportunity to draw the audience in with a detailed story. The basic lesson is they might have the most well-built model (or startup idea), but if they cannot explain it or connect to the customer, it loses value.

Once they get the hang of it, assign them to build a model and user story for their product or service. A user story is defined as a detailed narrative of a customer using the product or service and all its various functions from start to finish. I tell them they need to be intentional about the pieces they select whether shape, functionality or color because it adds depth to their description and story. There are sets available like Lego Serious Play aimed more toward businesses, but don't buy them! They are way too expensive. Ask around first, sometimes people have bins of them that have been sitting for years, but eBay or Craigslist is a great resource for old Legos. I bought a big lot on eBay and then washed them in a little bleach and water solution. Definitely worth the investment. If you are fortunate enough to get reimbursed, then you can get a lot more on eBay. If you are looking to buy, make sure there is a good mix of different bricks, movement pieces and figurines. If Legos are not an option, clay or Play-Doh can also achieve a similar effect.

17 CLOCK MANAGEMENT: PROJECT MANAGEMENT SOFTWARE

Some of the many blessings of technology are all the tools available to make life easier. When managing a team and a complex and ambitious project why not use technology? Trello (trello.com) is a fantastic project management tool. There are others out there like BaseCamp that have educational discounts, but Trello is free for their base model and has a great app, and is easy to learn. I will usually invite the students to my Trello and make it viewable for the class. I like this because you can follow their progress and it gives some context so you can coach them along. You can also have them sign up on their own and invite you to their project, but I like the flexibility of being an admin. I also pre-populate cards with the Business Model Canvas and then a list of their project deliverables with dates. I also include a list for: "Completed" "For Review" "In Progress" "Up Next" and "Questions/Roadblocks". Doing this work up front for them can minimize the Trello learning curve.

18 BUSINESS PROBLEMS

If you are able to recruit some local businesses to participate, this is a wonderful opportunity. The objective is for small businesses to propose a problem and the students (in teams) will work through a thorough business model to solve the problem. The emphasis is on "getting out of the building" to talk to customers. The end goal is to actually pitch their solutions to the business.

Here is what to look for in a business:
Businesses should urgently want to solve a problem of how to do something new that is rooted in questions about how customers respond.

The problem should be a B-to-C (business to consumer) problem because high school students do not have the business background to understand a B-to-B well enough to do deep problem-solving in the span of a few weeks. Also, students will need to complete substantial market research by interviewing real people. A B-to-B problem requires students to understand and research a market that is too specialized for them to get depth of understanding in a few weeks.

Owner/CEO should be a role model for the students. Being given a real problem facing a business by its owner/CEO is extremely motivating for students.

The problem needs to be substantive enough that there is a lot of room for creativity, allowing for a variety of ideas, approaches, and solutions between groups.

The problem is broad but well-defined and focused enough. Areas of uncertainty leave room for creativity yet if a problem is too big or too open-ended, students can struggle for too long to find a direction.

The problem targets a market that is sizeable and locally accessible. The students are expected to do deep market research, including interviewing of people. Even when 'leaving the building' is not possible, students can conduct interviews using phones or computers, also using emails and surveys to supplement. If the overall potential target market is too small, too specific, or is inaccessible to the students, they will struggle to produce meaningful data and feedback to guide their solution design. Anything that makes the research too constrained will severely restrict the students from being able to do their work effectively.

The business intends to scale. Ideally, the business wants to scale, even if only in theory. This is important because the research and problem-solving are only rich enough if the business is hoping to replicate and expand what they're doing. Startups with a vision for scale have to address elements like product-market fit, value propositions, customer segments, systems integration and solution validation, providing rich learning terrain for skills and knowledge that is broadly applicable.

Timing needs to be right. Sometimes it may look like a perfect fit, but the urgent problem they are facing may not be customer or market-related. In those cases, it is better to put the problem on the back burner until the timing of your problems better aligns with where the students are in the learning process.

Process

The class meets with the business owner/CEO, who presents the selected problem(s), usually with an in-depth debriefing so the students can fully understand the challenge and need for solutions. Some business problems will be large enough that all students work on the same problem, whereas others will have separate challenges assigned to different teams.

Once the problem has been given, the class will be divided into teams. We assign students to different teams for each business problem so that we maximize the learning each semester. The assignments are typically based on making sure each student works with as large a diversity of students as possible. No matter the personalities, strengths, previous relationships, or any other characteristic - simply putting students on very different teams for each problem will make for a lot of learning about collaboration, self, strengths, teaming, communications, etc.

After the teams are assembled, the first thing the students

learn about is product-market fit and how to do good market research. They learn this by diving deep into the research process. First, they must familiarize themselves with the problem, the market, specific terminology and any gaps surrounding the challenge or their understanding of it. This is done through secondary research with books and online resources.

Next, they begin to formulate customer archetypes and then go out into the real world and interview people, testing those archetypes. The teams continue to refine the problem based on feedback from interviews but have not formulated a solution yet.

As questions arise during the market research process, we will occasionally engage the business to provide answers to specific questions. Our rule is that each team is permitted a maximum of one email of questions to the business per 24 hours, requesting that businesses respond within 24 hours. When multiple teams have questions on the same day, we encourage teams to collect their questions into a single daily email with questions compiled from the class so as not to inundate the owner with communications from multiple students. But because the problems and the work is so externally-focused, the reality is that there are relatively few emails written to CEOs during the projects.

At the end of the each week, teams must present progress to the class. Each team must address the following statements in some way, though they are free to do so in whatever form or order they choose:

This is what we thought
This is what we did
This is what we learned
This is what we are doing next
This is what we are keeping in mind.

Only classmates attend this presentation and the atmosphere is casual compared to the final presentation made with the business owner or CEO in attendance. Teams typically have 5 minutes to present (with a hard stop), followed by a question and answer period. Students are not permitted to use note cards or outlines. Therefore, each presentation must be rehearsed enough to be complete but not memorized. While one team is presenting, the other students are engaged in live feedback that is accessible to the rest of the students and is discussed in the feedback and assessment section. In essence, while the team is presenting, the other students are typing anecdotal comments and questions into a shared document. Later, each team can review the comments made by their classmates and consider how they want to present their message going forward.

Students begin to create wireframes or mockups, testing and validating their solution with more customer interviews.

Students continually refine their customer archetypes, seeking the pain points and iterating towards a solution using the feedback from interviews and further research

The problem and the deadline become real as the business owner/CEO will be present for the team's final presentation. There is no "extension" and the teams know this. The owner of the business counts on the students for real solutions to their real problem. No matter what, the teams must present on this final day. The stakes are high and the students are motivated beyond the letter grade.

Teams are given typically 8 or 9 minutes to present, with 3-5 minutes for question and answer by the business CEO and team. Because students have been working to solve a problem for the business, questions from the rest of the audience are not allowed (they can stay after the presentations and ask teams questions if they wish).

After the four teams present, the business owner or CEO meets with each team individually for 15 minutes so that teams can give the CEO more of their research and findings (often prepared in the form of a handout). This also allows the business time for additional questions and discussion with the team about their solution.

Another alternative to the business problem is by proposing a social one. Identify an issue in the world and ask the students to solve it and pitch. For instance, you may give the students a project to solve famine in East Africa. Or how should you rebuild Puerto Rico after a devastating hurricane? This requires an extensive interdisciplinary approach and still builds on the same skills of traditional startups. This sort of project can seem overwhelming and may be difficult for buy-in, especially if students are thinking of their own ideas they want to pursue. The key is the project set-up and having an end goal. If at all possible, have a speaker come in who is working with an NGO solving these problems or is an expert in it to set up the problem for the students and to be present for the final presentation.

Finally, you can also use a context most students are familiar with—and that is their own school or institution. I have used this before and have found it to be pretty successful. Students feel like they have more skin in the game and there is more of an interest in solving a problem directly benefiting them and their peers. This is also fun because you can invite school administrators to be on the panel as this gives them a chance to get in touch with students. The problem to solve could be efficiency related or a business opportunity within the school. During one of these projects I had a student wanting to rethink and redesign the school uniform, specifically the skirt. She invented a new design and prototype and found validation in this phase and used it as her startup idea. She parlayed her experience into a new skirt business to market to private schools!

19 MENTORS AND SPEAKERS

One of the best parts of this course will be the utilization of outside speakers and mentors. There is efforting up front to find good speakers who can make time to visit, but it is well worth the time investment. The key is to try and diversify your speakers. Bringing in three different insurance salespeople might yield a few different pearls of wisdom, but will not have the intended effect. I was concerned initially that people would not want to give up their time, but I found the vast majority of professionals want to give back and share their insight and be helpful. The key piece of advice is to make sure they are ok coming in *pro bono*. 99% of the time it is not even a question, but there were a couple times I assumed and I was wrong.

If there are areas you are weak on in the business realm use those weaknesses to focus your search for finding your speakers. For instance, I know I am weak on business law and IP (intellectual property) so I make sure I bring in someone to talk about those aspects in a way which is accessible to my students. I then can draw from the speaker the rest of the course.

Some of my favorite outside of the box speakers I have had the privilege of bringing in was a magician, and an improv professional. These are all entrepreneurs in perhaps unconventional ways but the magician was able to discuss how to market himself and stay passionate while doing a few killer tricks. The improv professional taught us how to say yes by being willing to take risks (in life and improv), how being vulnerable creates amazing art, and the openness to go down a different path can yield rewards. We also did some improv games together and it was so much fun.

I also use outside help for mentorship, especially with the student startup project. I will try and find a lunch hour where I can get all the mentors to come in and I require the students to show up as well. I flip the script and have the mentors come in and take two minutes to pitch themselves and then the student teams will pick their mentor for the project. This makes more sense than the mentors selecting the teams because in the real business and nonprofit world, the board is chosen and voted in. I let the mentors know their involvement is completely up to them. The bare minimum is 1 email exchange a week. Most have the bandwidth for that and many of them are even more generous with their time. Be aware of any mentors "gravy-training" the students. I have had projects where a mentor has played the role of "generous uncle" and has given some startup money, but then required equity without doing much work in return. It is probably best to keep mentors as mentors, and not as investors. If they have rolodex help, then that can be explored with caution.

20 THE THANK YOU NOTE

The thank you note is a bit of a lost art. You can play around with how you want to encourage this mindset. You can model it from the front whereby you create a class thank you card and have everyone sign it. I carve a couple minutes at the end of an in-class speaker to get a group photo with the guest and then print it to Target or Costco and include the photo along with the class thank you note. This is usually the method which makes most sense with a speaker, otherwise you send a lot of mail if each student writes their own note. If you want the students to get into the habit personally, sometimes a written note does not make sense for them, but a thank you email does. Whatever fits your personality and beliefs on the matter. Either way, the thank you note is not a negotiable. I also believe encouraging students to shake the hand of the speaker and introduce themselves and say thank you for their time (even if they disagreed with them) is also the right thing to do.

21 STUDENT STARTUP

This is the last project or capstone and most likely what
the students had in mind when they signed up for the
class. Students finally get a chance to come up with their
own startup idea, form teams, and work through the
business model to pitch to actual investors (if possible). I
have the students read *Disciplined Entrepreneurship* and
again the students email me the most salient or
enlightening aspect of the chapter and how they will
implement it in their startup. I also have the teams
complete the steps via detoolbox.com so that they are
getting the content at least twice. At the end of each
grouping, they are required to do a quick stand up
presentation (with deck) to talk through their findings and
receive feedback from their peers. This method allows
for the students to get more and more comfortable up in
front of people speaking and fielding questions. This also
helps to shape their business model. If you notice below,
I have chopped up the book to fit my course, but the
book is already designed for the reader to go in numerical
order or by themes, so do what makes most sense for
you.

Business Model: read and complete *Disciplined
Entrepreneurship* Steps 1, 2, 4, 11
Value Proposition: read and complete *Disciplined
Entrepreneurship* Steps 7, 8, 10, 22, 23
Customer Segments: read and complete *Disciplined
Entrepreneurship* Steps 3, 5, 9

Channels & Partners: read and complete *Disciplined Entrepreneurship* Steps 6, 12, 13
Customer Relationships: read and complete *Disciplined Entrepreneurship* Steps 17, 18, 19, 20, 21
Revenue Streams: read and complete *Disciplined Entrepreneurship* Steps 15, 16
Resources, Costs, Activities: read and complete *Disciplined Entrepreneurship* Steps 14, 24

Wireframe or Prototype

I require the teams to have a tangible prototype of their product, or a wireframe if it is an app or website (ie: bubble.is or mockflow.com), or at least a video if it is a service. Even a scrappy prototype is helpful. I had a team with an innovative backpack idea and it wasn't until they built the prototype that other peers and their own mentor finally understood the vision. The group explained it as well as they could but it wasn't translating, so this is a critical step for all the stakeholders.

Website

I require the students to publish a basic website and most students will use the free Wix version to do so. I try to encourage students who have never built a website before to be the ones who build it so they can learn. For those in the group who are the tech gurus, it is a great opportunity for them to learn to coach without micromanaging. I never require them to purchase a domain or servers or a WYSIWYG builder (Squarespace or premium Wix), but some will do it on their own.

Regardless, a discussion on URLs (web real estate) and SEO is helpful either in class or as it comes up.

The pitch deck, telling a story and final pitch

I give students a presentation deck rubric with minimum required slides and I also show examples for them to glean ideas from. I emphasize less is more and that design matters—the impression you give from the first slide onward (clean, clear, no spelling errors) has a substantial impact on investors and panelists. I always reject a Prezi and reduce their options to a PowerPoint, Google Slides or a PDF.

If it all possible, I believe the team with the best story and energy will place well. Your numbers could be a little shaky but it is not the unpardonable sin when you pitch, especially if you communicate the model well. One way to help them shape their story is *The Karate Kid* approach. Daniel-San is lost and bullied. He meets a teacher, a guru Mr. Miyagi who gives him the tools (in exchange for a bunch of free labor) to address his problem of lack of confidence and bullies. His call to action is fighting in a tournament to stop the bullying by using these tools which leads to a tournament victory, no more bullies and he gets the girl! This is the typical plot we are accustomed to and a great template for students struggling to communicate their idea. Who is your Daniel-San (customer) and what is their problem? How are you Mr. Miyagi? What tools are you providing or what problem are you solving? What is Daniel-San's (your customers) call to action? What value will it end up providing in the end?

As much as you can create a special event around this final presentation, the better. I try to organize a Pitch Night in the early evening, invite the school community and arrange for some inexpensive catering. If you can find some local angels or VC's to sit on the panel, that would be best. This is not a "Shark Tank" event where the panel is offering money for equity, but they are there to evaluate the business model and provide meaningful feedback. It is critical to let them know what they (the panel) should be looking for, so make sure you have expectations to match your goals and objectives. Typically, pitch competitions are weighed heavily on business model, design (MVP) and customer validation. As for other logistics, depending on how many teams you have is probably how you want to set the presentation schedule. You don't really want to go past the 2 hour threshold, so keep the pitches to a 5-10 minute range (less is more) and 3-5 minutes for questions. A few other notes I have picked up along the way is to require the teams to submit their pitch decks early to force presentation practice. Younger students tend to under-practice. In terms of a tech backup, I save all their decks in a PDF format on a flash drive in addition to the cloud just in case something goes wrong. A simple "tech check" 30 minutes prior will usually eliminate wasted time and allow for quick troubleshooting.

The Debrief

Once again after the final pitches we do a retrospective for the entire project, but I also have them complete a "360 review" on their whole team. Each team member is to be evaluated. Essentially this is an opportunity for students to get some closure and vent, especially if they had people on their team not living up to their agreements. It is up to you how much you want to weight this. I typically still defer to what they set in their agreements or bylaws. Since it is common for student groups to agree "we all get the same grade regardless" this outlet to speak their mind can be helpful even when students feel a sense of inequity in the grade.

22 SOCIAL ENGAGEMENTS

"Rats and roaches live by competition under the law of supply and demand; it is the privilege of human beings to live under the laws of justice and mercy." - Wendell Berry

Incorporating social responsibility into the class or program should not be forced or taught as an add-on. It is obvious when companies attempt to do this, so why do this in the class? Social responsibility makes more sense when it is organically tied to a business' mission and values. It is unfortunate social good is manipulated by some businesses eager to capitalize on tragedy and even some NGO's are turning into a racket. Social responsibility is a very worthy topic to discuss but the more Socratic in approach and tied into their personal and company values, the better.

One option prior to forming startups is to look at various case studies and asking about unintended consequences such as, when does helping actually cause damage? Or to get a feel for the class you could ask an anonymous index card question like, "what makes a company social responsible?" For instance, if a company hosts several high earning 5k events for children's cancer, but uses sweatshop labor for their products, does this make them socially responsible or not?

I personally believe every business should have social responsibility built into its core values, and with social media there is a cost to not being socially responsible. Some great case studies of social businesses for better or worse are of course, TOMS Shoes (I recommend the Tim Ferriss interview with Blake Mycoskie as a good resource if short on time, otherwise *Start Something that Matters* by Blake Mycoskie is a nice primer on the business). A further investigation could be how difficult it is to actually make good on the promise to give back? For instance, how much cost is involved and what is the supply chain to give TOMS shoes away in a third world village? How does it impact the local economy?

Bombas socks (bombas.com) is another "1-for-1" business model to consider since socks are always in need at homeless shelters (they also appeared on Shark Tank). Rareform (rareform.com), another Shark Tank business takes billboard waste and repurposes the material into innovative bags and products. Patagonia (patagonia.com) is another case study (*Let My People Go Surfing* by Yvon Chouinard is a fun read). I also highly suggest on the social enterprise front, Homeboy Industries (homeboyindustries.org). The documentary, *G-Dog* explains the story of Homeboy Industries and is well worth the time and discussion, not just in terms of philosophy, but also business model and structure. There will be plenty of students that want to make a difference with their startup and it is not uncommon for them to consider the nonprofit route. These case studies can help to inform the students about corporate structure options and the pros and cons of each.

A great activity to get the students to think about their own core values is by doing a group simulation. Here is the activity to modify as you see fit:

You are a portfolio manager for a wealthy client. This client inherited shares in 6 different companies and is not interested in investing in new ones. The client also wants to be more ethically responsible in her investments. She has an even $100,000 invested in each company and says "money really isn't an issue, but still wants to do well in the market." Your task is to remove two companies from her portfolio and double-down on two others. After researching each company's track record and values, which companies will you remove from her portfolio and which two will you increase investment in?

Facebook (FB)
Hooters [Chanticleer Holdings; (BURG)]
Amazon (AMZN)
Coca-Cola (KO)
McDonalds (MCD)
Old Navy [Gap Inc.; GPS)]

This particular activity can last several class sessions and involves higher level thinking. I usually have each student privately do their own research and come to their own decision first. I reiterate they are to be careful from where they get their information and should be able to not only cite their sources but do their best to vet the information. Once this is completed, then at their table or group with their decision they will have a team discussion and come to a group consensus.

Once they arrive at a group or team consensus, I then open it up to the whole class and aim for total class consensus. I have each team or table give their vote and rationale. I write the stocks on the board and make tally marks so they can visually see the class voting. As a result, individual values start to emerge and heated but great conversations ensue. Again, this activity can get very emotional and so it is critical to keep their composure by affirming their stance, but also encouraging them to articulate why they value what they do. After the class conversation, consensus or not, you can also have them reset the activity, but they have to start first by listing their non-negotiables. In other words, what behaviors will they have a zero-tolerance for? Once these behaviors or activities are listed, have them go through the process again and see if the results change based on this framework. The main objective of this simulation is to identify assumed values, the importance of defining values up front instead of "on the fly" and learning how to engage diverse values/opinions.

Finally, I usually have the students write their team startup agreement including their Mission Statement, Vision and Values. This exercise makes the values discussion more organic.

23 STARTUP WEEKEND OR HACKATHON

There are several opportunities for students (and the teacher) to be a part of various pitch competitions throughout the year and they are all valuable. I have come to really appreciate StartUp Weekends (startupweekend.org) and Hackathons. I always encourage my students to participate, and while I do not get a lot of students sign up because of their busy schedules, the students who can participate always walk away changed for the better. I had a student from a previous history class taking entrepreneurship with me and he was the type of student who didn't turn work in on time, and the quality was usually average at best. He was a thoughtful student and smart, but from the vantage point of a teacher he was lazy. He signed up for the local StartUp Weekend event and I greeted him and was his wingman throughout the weekend. The team he joined was welcoming and he was immediately viewed as a valuable asset and his youth was never looked down upon. The project involved blockchain technology which was completely new to him but he engaged and worked hard to contribute in ways he could. This alone was empowering to him but the overall transformation from that weekend was noteworthy. Not only did he learn more about startups, entrepreneurship and about himself than from a whole year of class, he also changed his demeanor when class resumed. Immediately he was more engaged, wanted to discuss entrepreneurial things, he turned work in on time, and in some cases early! He also assumed and volunteered for leadership roles when the opportunity presented itself.

Another success story was a young female student winning the People's Choice Award for her pitch on underwater photography goggles. She is a gifted musician and that is her wheelhouse, but she was willing to be stretched and take risks and was rewarded with participants affirming and encouraging her and she inspired my own class when she returned on Monday. Obviously your results may vary and this is not normal, but the point remains I have not had a student disappointed they participated in these events.

24 INCUBATOR PARTNERSHIPS AND SCHOOL RELATIONSHIPS

One of the biggest value-adds our entrepreneurship program provides is that we are not on an island but connected to other entrepreneurship programs. We have been fortunate to develop a partnership with a local incubator and coworking space, Hub 101 (hub101.la). In our case, we are extremely lucky because our school is only a half a mile away. In addition, this particular incubator is underwritten by a local university (specifically, The California Lutheran Center for Entrepreneurship, callutheran.edu) which also believes academia and entrepreneurship are not mutually exclusive. Their willingness to be inclusive of young entrepreneurs, accessible to the community at-large, student-centric and academic has allowed for a burgeoning community which otherwise would have been stunted due to only hosting well-funded startups. Almost reminiscent of the "penny universities" during the Enlightenment, where students would ditch their classes to hang out in the coffeehouses to learn from those actually creating and experimenting, first time startup students are able to work alongside seasoned entrepreneurs, seek advice, mentorship, and learn best practices. The center actively hosts events and speakers and our students have access to those extra-curricular opportunities as well. I had one student with a decent social media business invited to speak at the center as a part of their distinguished speaker series.

I make it an assignment to visit the center at the beginning of the year to introduce themselves, get a tour, and finally take a selfie so I know they went. A great portion of students feel as though they have stumbled upon a hidden secret and I say, "I know, that's why I made you go as an assignment. Now go and use it."

When our program was being created, our first conversation was with the School of Management at California Lutheran University which oversees the Entrepreneurship courses. We designed our curriculum based on what they do. There is a slight difference in rigor, but not much. We have worked so closely in terms of curriculum that the University and our school created a dual-credit agreement so our students in high school can earn college credit for their work in the high school entrepreneurship class. If you are able to connect with an entrepreneurship program at another school and/or at a local incubator, it will be an iron sharpening iron effect and can greatly improve the value and experience of the class for you, your students, and for the incubator/accelerator or University.

25 HOW TO FIND A PASSION OR IDEA

There will inevitably be students struggling to find a startup idea. They desperately want to, but can't seem to really know what they want to do. Completely understandable. In some cases it is because they have so many things they could do. First, I think it is important to let them know they do not have to settle on one idea. They should try as many things as they can without disrupting too much of their bandwidth, or other responsibilities. But even with that stress addressed, they still want to tap into their desires.

One of my favorite questions is to inquire about their childhood imagination, daydreams, or favorite childhood book. This is not researched but simply anecdotal. I have learned from my students over the years that the intersection of gifts and desires were already present from childhood, but the expectations of society, school, parents, friends and even self-imposed expectations have beaten it out of them. Asking students to explain what their go-to imaginative play scenarios were when they played with friends as a kid can unlock some things for them. This of course does not mean that if they pretended to be Spider-Man that they are destined to be bitten by a radioactive spider. It is what is behind the desire. A desire to save, help, or serve others may actually be illuminating to them. My favorite example is a student who was a great student academically and was on track to go to Notre Dame and study business. At first glance, we would say this is a dream scenario for many, and he is most certainly setting himself up to be successful in life. However, he was not really himself and not very content when studying business at Notre Dame. He moved back to Los Angeles and started to pursue acting. Most people would suggest this is selfish and foolish. But he put everything into it, did the work, and was truly happy. I asked him what he did as a kid with his friends and he said, "oh, me and my friends would always make stupid short films." Interesting. His father was a very successful businessman who had also attended Notre Dame. While the father would never force it, the son felt obligated, perhaps subconsciously, to follow in his dad's footsteps. Those expectations eroded that natural and innate joy from childhood of acting and making films with his friends.

If this question is too hard for them, then ask what they would typically daydream about in school. I believe daydreams are a vital part of the curriculum—unintended and unwritten of course—but since we are not designed to sit in air conditioned buildings all day, the daydream can be our soul reminding us of our true calling. I would rather students daydream and creatively use their own imagination than stare at a screen and have their imagination commandeered by feeds. Again, if this question is lost on them, you can ask about an all-time favorite childhood book and inquire about why that book was so meaningful. What is it about the story or the characters or drawings, etc. The main point is their calling and desire is most likely already inside them and simply needs to be revealed after cutting away the brush and weeds of expectations.

Another leading question to help them discover an idea is to ask them what sort of things make them angry. Anger is such a powerful emotion and can stay in our system for days. It is up to us to channel that anger to not destroy us or others but to use the energy to drive us to solve a very real problem. If we are frustrated by it, then there are invariably others who are frustrated by it as well. As Kevin Kelly suggests, if you can find 1-in-a-million to side with you, then you can potentially make a living.

Finally, sometimes there are just creative roadblocks. I cannot recommend enough *The War of Art* by Steven Pressfield. It is a fast read and is worth having a copy on hand in your classroom. In many cases having a student plough through that book will be enough to get them started.

26 SELF-AWARENESS

In addition to finding an idea, students are in a period of finding themselves and forming identities (actually, aren't we all?). In addition to exploring childhood desires, some online tools can be helpful to encourage and affirm their strengths.

The classic Myers-Briggs can be helpful, but I tend to like the depth StrengthsFinder (strengths.gallup.com) and Enneagram can provide. The tests aid to identify how and why we think, feel, and lead the way we do, and can help make group work a little more functional. StrengthsFinder will run you about $10 a test and for most schools and teachers this is not feasible. You might be able to consider it a textbook for the students to buy, but is probably only worth it if you can find a StrengthsFinder trainer or if you invest some time in understanding it yourself and then utilize it throughout the course. If you cannot find the means for StrengthsFinder, the other option is the Enneagram test which has both paid and free versions. If Enneagram is new to you, there is plenty of free literature online. The free version is very suitable and enlightening (eclecticenergies.com/enneagram/test).

These tests can be helpful in your encouragement of students, and gives them some vocabulary to describe and understand themselves better. If you don't have time or don't really care for personality tests, that is totally fine.

But if at all possible, whenever you have a chance to introduce a student to someone, aim to introduce them as what they are. "This is Tommy, he is an entrepreneur and artist." "This is Laura, she is an activist and writer." "This is Colin, he is one of our most innovative apparel entrepreneurs and a philanthropist." It is amazing the power our words have on our students and sometimes your affirmation can be all the personality test they ever need.

27 PUBLIC SPEAKING PRACTICE

While this play might be better suited for a speech class, there is always a need for public speaking practice and this can be a fun and easy drill for students to practice speaking. Have a student stand up front, give them a basic topic and let them talk about it for two minutes (maybe use those Snake Oil cards again). Or you can give students a basic item and have them talk about the features and benefits of the item. For instance, something simple like a roll of toilet paper can yield several of them. If students are not comfortable alone, then you can modify by having two students up front and asking them to have a conversation about a random topic to facilitate practicing listening and asking and sharing. Another possible book recommendation to incorporate or to glean some tips is *Public Speaking and Influencing Men in Business*, by Dale Carnegie.

28 THE RESUME

As the year or the class comes to a close, I require an assignment where the students create their resume or CV. In my experience, 95% of students don't even have one yet, so it is a great gift for them as they can now simply revise it the rest of their life. I wait until the end of the course because I have them put their startup on the resume (whether they succeeded it or not).

I am honest with them that in most cases people are not hired because they have an amazing resume, but you still need to have one. In many cases it is an indirect hire (someone vouched for you, or you knew someone, or you were an internal hire) which is estimated at around 80% of hires. Therefore, I encourage students to play the numbers game and seek out relationships. I constantly stress that our education system is built to sell a dream. There is a belief that you cannot really get started on a career until you have a college degree. I tell them if they have the slightest clue of what they want to do, go and find the people doing the things they want to do and get in. This might mean begging to work for free, an internship, or a meeting to pick their brain, or sit in meetings to take notes. This will be a bigger advantage in the long run than solely a prestigious degree. Obviously, the more options the better so they should pursue both, but I would argue an amazing degree + an entitled student = disappointment; whereas average degree +

motivated student = opportunities.

Here are resume notes I give in addition to a full example:

- Save the file with your Name (example: Debbie Downer Resume; DebbieDowner_CV, etc.) not just "Resume"
- Design/Layout matters. It's often your first impression to a recruiter or a future boss. Make sure it is professional but reflects your personality
- Order your jobs/activities in reverse chronological order (most recent first)
- Make it "scanable" (easy to read)
- Differentiate the name of the company/and timeframe with bold font, etc.
- Use bullets. No one in the business world has time to read paragraphs
- Start every bullet with a verb for consistency and to demonstrate action
- Try to use numbers to quantify the results of your efforts as much as you can
- Create an intro section or summary if possible (See example: "black belt" in sales enablement to make it a little fun) and use of numbers to make it easy to read)
- Extracurricular activities are great to include, but make sure you demonstrate what you've learned or contributed
- Spellcheck! Make sure you're using periods

consistently
- 1 page only

Depending on time, I will also have the students create a LinkedIn profile and also create a contact card on their smartphone with their picture and other details so when they exchange a contact, there will be context and details to follow up on.

29 HUMANITIES APPROACH

As mentioned, the more humanities you can incorporate the better. It is never a waste in an entrepreneurship class, but its execution is vital. Built on the assumption entrepreneurship is a sport and meant to be played, it is not wise (not to mention a disappointment) to do a purely theoretical class. Again, this class is an opportunity to transform imaginations and explore their human potential. Use things you are comfortable with. If you have an affinity for Ayn Rand's *The Fountainhead*, then use it. Trying to force a text you haven't read and don't care about will negate any attempt at infusing a humanities approach to entrepreneurship. That said, here are a couple suggestions to get the mind going as you begin to craft your unique syllabus or course.

Texts:

Man's Search For Meaning by Viktor Frankl. This book should act as the *de facto* grid before launching into a new venture or class. If are aren't familiar, the context is Dr. Frankl's personal experience in a concentration camp during World War 2 and his insights from working with survivors after liberation. The perspective it offers on finding redemption and coping with suffering by finding a meaningful project is priceless and is also helpful for the student looking for meaning and purpose in their own startup and lives.

Brave New World by Huxley perhaps followed up by *Amusing Ourselves to Death* by Neil Postman. Dystopian literature can lend itself to thinking about entrepreneurship in a holistic and consequentialist way, and hopefully driving you back to core values. This type of reading allows us to ask, "what kind of world will this product or service create?" If you are a Netflix aficionado, *Black Mirror* could also yield some supplemental content for dystopian thinking and discussion.

How Will You Measure Your Life? by Clayton M. Christensen. Originally an article in HBR, and actually might be more suitable to use with time constraints, focuses in on the importance of taking the time to discover your life's purpose and considering a different metric to judge success beyond bottom lines.

Philosophy:

Discussion on Nietzsche's *Will to Power* or Machiavellian thought (*The Prince*) coupled with the Star Power Game Simulation (simulationtrainingsystems.com). The simulation is a powerful illustration. It is essentially a trading game where the rules of the game get to be changed by the most powerful group. It is a great conversation on privilege, human nature and greed. You can buy it (expensive) or try and make your own. Even without the simulation, Nietzsche's argument that the sole drive for humans is power can be illuminating and a great class discussion.

Social Science:

The Challenge of Affluence: Self-Control and Well-Being in the United States and Britain since 1950 by Avner Offer. A definite check in our spirit about our intended or unintended affluence and wealth creation. The book argues prudence helped us to become affluent, but in affluence prudence is eroded away and leads, eventually back into poverty of the mind and wallet. If short on time, even just reading his thesis or introduction is sufficient for a conversation.

History:

Casey Neistat (filmmaker) has been quoted, "I think I learned everything I know about business and life from reading about World War 2." This is a great starting point for students to research and identify what aspects from World War 2 are actually helpful in business. I haven't found any syllabus available on this, but could be an incredible class to create!

Documentaries:

Century of the Self, Adam Curtis. Great to couple with Psychology (Freud), but the larger context is to think about marketing and its ethics. *Propaganda* by Ellul (advanced reading) or Bernays (same title) could be a nice and challenging supplement as well.

Enron: The Smartest Guys in the Room (Again a discussion on ethics and also how worldviews like Social Darwinism shape decisions and businesses).

Film:

Seven Samurai, Akira Kurosawa (long, old and foreign but a very good opportunity to discuss leadership and teams)

In general, a study of story and plot structure can be fundamental in communication and marketing. Campbell's *The Hero with a Thousand Faces* or Robert McKee's *Story* can be also be beneficial.

The amount of time you have will never be enough, but even just one intentional use of some outside text or philosophy or history is worth making time for. One of the easiest ways is to make an intentional effort to partner with another teacher or another department to collaborate and organically weave humanities in with entrepreneurship. The process in itself will be entrepreneurial for the teachers and fun.

30 LAUNCH!

If you plan to create and teach an entrepreneurship class, don't be afraid to try new things and make mistakes. Be honest and upfront with students. A great teacher doesn't simply "push content" but asks great questions and acts more like an agent or a coach than a gatekeeper. This course is all about facilitating thoughtful, articulate, creative, critical thinking, loving, imaginative, problem-solving leaders. This can aid in their transformation from overconsumption into confidence, and foster a healthier mindset. This is hard work, but necessary work and valuable work. It requires patience, frustration, and sacrifice. This ultimately has nothing to do with new small business creation but everything to do with their character, integrity, human potential, purpose and being fantastic stewards of their resources—the planet, their own hearts, minds, souls as well as those people they are privileged to interact with. This is the bottom-line and the measuring stick for success. And if these same students also enjoy the by-products and monetization that can come with entrepreneurial success, even better.

As the world is changing there is no better time to install or improve on your entrepreneurship program to compete in the educational marketplace, but also to properly, compassionately, and intelligently invest in the next generation.

APPENDIX: EGG DROP PROJECT

Objective: Yolks and Folks Corp. is looking for a company which can drop eggs from the second floor outside to the concrete ground without breakage and provide the best value.

Your team will follow a modified Design Sprint.

Budget = $75

You may only purchase supplies from the 'market' (me). You will need to fill out a purchase order for each time you make a purchase.

Test as much as you need, but don't go over budget. And you should have enough money left to do one final drop for the pitch to me.

You will give a quick pitch to me on why your group has the best egg droppage method/product for the best value.

You don't necessarily have to be the least expensive, but it is definitely taken into consideration.

Things to include in pitch: (You may use slide presentations but it is not required.)
Your company name (tagline optional)
Your evidence/data on why I should trust your product.
What your product is made of/process.
Actual live drop in front of me.
How much you charge for each drop (the egg IS included in the price, you provide the egg). Don't forget to make some margin or profit on the drop.

<u>Market Value:</u>
Painters Tape – 1 ft. $1
Balloons (uninflated) – $1
Brown Lunch Bag – $1 each
Pipe cleaners – 2 for $1
Newspaper sheet - $1 each
Rubberbands – 10 for $1
Cardstock – $1 each
Ribbon – $1 each
Paper Towel Square – 2 squares $1
Non-Latex Gloves - $1 each
Eggs - $5

APPENDIX: THE BUSINESS LICENSE EXAM

In order to participate in selling for the $20 project you need to pass the BLE (Business License Exam). The test is purely a term literacy and its application test and not an actual government mandated test. There are 100ish terms you should know well, but this list is not definitive for class or in start-ups. You must score at least an 80% on the test to pass. You may retake as many times as you like until you pass. The score you get goes in the grade book. If you score an 82, but wish to retake later, you may. The test is multiple choice.

"In the black"
"In the red"
1-to-1 Marketing
A/B testing
A Round financing
Adjacent market
Agile sprint
Angel Investors
Assets
Barriers to Entry
Bootstrapping
Break-Even
Brick and Mortar
Bridge Loan
Burn Rate
Business-to-Business (B-to-B or B2B)
Business-to-Consumer (B-to-C or B2C)

Business Model Canvas (and its 9 parts)
Capital
Cash Flow
CEO
CFO
Channels (distribution)
COGS (cost of goods and services)
Competitive Advantage
Conflict of Interest
COO
CPM (ad clicks)
Crowdfunding
Customer acquisition cost
Customer Archetypes
Debt
Demographics

Direct Marketing
Due Diligence
Earnings Before Interest, Taxes, Depreciation, and Amortization (EBITDA)
Elevator Pitch
Entrepreneurial Arbitrage
Equity stake
Exit strategy
Gross Profit
Guerrilla Marketing
Incubator
Influencer Marketing
Intellectual Property
Inventory
Invoice
Lead Time
Lean Start-Up
Limited Liability Company (LLC)
Liquidity
Marketability
Metrics
Minimum viable product (MVP)
Monetize
NDA (non-disclosure agreement)
Net Profit
Niche Market
Operating Budget
Operating Expense

Operating Income
Opportunity Cost
Outsourcing
Overhead costs
Patent
Per Capita
pivot
Private Equity
Pro Forma
Profit and Loss (P&L) Statement
Profit Margin
Profit Sharing
Project Management
Proof of Concept
Prototype
Rate of Return
Research and development (R&D)
Return on Investment (ROI)
Revenue
Royalties
Saturation (product)
Scale/scalability
Seed Money/Capital
Served/Serviceable Available Market (SAM)
Sole Proprietorship
Stakeholders
Stockholder or Shareholder
Supply Chain
Sustainability

Sweat Equity
SWOT Analysis
Target
Market/Customer
Time-to-Market
Total Available
(addressable) Market
(TAM)

UI Designer
UX Designer
Valuation
Value Add/Added
Value Proposition
Wholesale
Wireframe

APPENDIX: THE $20 PROJECT

Your team will be given an actual $20 investment from me (0% loan). Your task is to start a mini-business with only the capital given. YOU MAY NOT borrow any money, assets, or add your own money. You MAY however reinvest your profits into the business. If you are planning on using materials or equipment already owned, you have to get permission from me first.

You may begin selling ONLY once your whole team has earned their selling license. You may start working on marketing and strategies but you cannot order or start selling until all members have passed the test and earned their license.

Project Deliverables:

BMC - Complete a Business Model Canvas (remember this will change frequently)

Bylaws - Complete your bylaws (see Appendix: Bylaws for a template)

Lego User Story - Using Legos begin to tell a user story of your product or service and/or Product Elevator Pitch - Present your product or service to the class

Print Ad - Create a print ad for your product or service. It must include at the very least your DBA and contact information/social media.

Video Ad (Optional) - This requires some extra time and work but can be really fun.

Daily or Weekly Stand Up Reports - What did you work on, what will you work on, roadblocks?

All documentation and receipts - Everything needs to be accounted for. Receipts, sales, comps EVERYTHING!

Final Fundraising Deck - Create a deck and pitch asking for more funding.

Retrospective/Debrief - We will debrief your project and experience.

By participating, you agree that this project is purely for educational purposes and not intended to be an actual business. You understand this project is highly regulated and is set up only for a short period of time. You also understand any income/revenue may be returned to the original owners or customers or given to a charity of your choice.

APPENDIX: BYLAWS/STARTUP AGREEMENT FORMS

Bylaws of (Fictitious Business Name)

Article I
This business shall be known as (Enter DBA) and will be referred to in this document as (enter either DBA or FBN)

Article II
The purpose of _____ is [Write out what the purpose of what your mini-business is.]

Article III
The _____ consists of the following (Members and Roles. What is the name and title of each member of your team?)

Article III-A
Explanation of roles (Explain the role, responsibilities, expectations of each role. You do not need to have all of these but be thinking about ordering, sales, financials, record-keeping/documentation, treasurer, marketing/advertising, decision making, etc.)

Article IV
Meetings/Voting Policy
[Specifically, the bylaws should indicate who may call meetings, the place of the meetings and how directors and members are to be notified. Bylaws also should indicate how many members must be present for corporate action to occur, referred to as a quorum, and what constitutes a majority vote. An example might be

requiring a supermajority vote, meaning two-thirds majority. Or will it require a unanimous (100% agreement) vote. What will your tie-break policy be? The bylaws should also address whether action can be taken without meetings, and whether voting can be done without a member actually present, known as proxy voting.]

Article V
Compensation (grading rubric)
If someone in your team is not holding up their responsibilities, what will the grade deduction be for that individual? Or will everyone get the same grade regardless of unequal teamwork?

Article VI
We, the _____ and its members understand this is purely an educational opportunity and does not constitute a real business. We understand the final net income may be donated back to the class or given to a charity since this is an educational opportunity and not a registered or regulated business. We understand if we choose to continue with our product or service, we are required to become compliant with all necessary governmental and school institutions.

Each member needs to Sign and Date

Name
(Print)_____

Signed_____Date_____

Version 2: Student Start-Up Agreement

I. **Partnership name.** This will be the legal name of your partnership or Fictitious Business Name.
    a. **DBA** (Doing Business As)

II. **Business address.** This is the physical address for the partnership. If there is none or only a post office box, then choose the address for one of the partners

III. **Names of Partners.**

IV. **Effective date of agreement.** This is the date that the partnership will begin. The date should be shortly after the Partnership Agreement is signed by all the partners.

V. **Primary purpose of partnership.** For example, to start a particular business, or sell a product or service.
    a. To the best of your ability, outline the job or task or expectation for each partner (you may add the phrase "and any other responsibilities not listed.")
    b. List your company's Mission Statement, Company Vision and Company Values.

VI. **Ownership Amounts and Voting requirements for partnership decisions.** Generally, there are three options, including:
- all partners have equal voting rights regardless of ownership percentage (meaning each partner has one vote);
- all decisions require a majority vote with voting rights based on ownership percentage; or,

- all decisions require unanimous vote.

VII. **Specify how costs will be shared among the partners**. Typically this is according to ownership percentage. However, costs may also be assigned by percentages to each partner.

VIII. **Specify how profits will be shared among the partners**. Typically this is according to ownership percentage. However, profits may also be assigned by percentages to each partner.

IX. **Specify which partners will have authority to sign checks from the partnership account**.

X. **Specify who will maintain accounting of profits made by partnership**. Typically, this is an accountant or one of the partners. This may be an accounting firm or a person.

XI. If partner withdraws from partnership, **specify number of days the partnership, as an entity, will have to buy the withdrawn shares and how long a partner must be vested (time an employee must work before leaving with equity)**.

XII. **Specify type of vote required to dissolve partnership**. This may be unanimous, by a majority, single partner vote or some other method.

Partner (typed)

(signed)_____Date_____

NOTES:

Beau Brannan

ABOUT THE AUTHOR

Beau Brannan (M.A. Education) currently runs the entrepreneurship program at Oaks Christian School in Westlake Village, California. He has a humanities soul and an entrepreneurial mind. He enjoys traveling to Guatemala and leading delegations there. He spent years playing and coaching football and believes "the waggle" is the best play in football and can be found at brannan.tv

Beau Brannan